Published simultaneously in Canada and the USA by Cupress Ltd.
10 Falconer Drive, Unit 8, Mississauga, Ontario, L5N 1B1, Canada.

First published in 1986 by Lutterworth Press, Cambridge, England
with whose agreement this edition is published.

for FRITZ

Traditional English Melody

All things bright and beautiful, All creatures great and small,

All things wise and wonderful, The Lord God made them all.

Each little flower that opens, Each little bird that sings,

He made their glowing colours, He made their tiny wings.

British Library Cataloguing in Publication Data

Baynes, Pauline
  All things bright and beautiful.
  I. Title II. Alexander, Mrs C. F.
  264'.2 BV353

Illustrations copyright © 1986 Pauline Baynes

Music arrangement © Lutterworth Press 1986

Printed in Singapore

All Things Bright and Beautiful

words by
Cecil Frances Alexander
1818–1895

Illustrated by Pauline Baynes

98-1922

▲▲▲CUPRESS LTD.

All things bright and beautiful,
All creatures great and small,

All things wise and wonderful,
The Lord God made them all.

Each little flower that opens,
Each little bird that sings,

He made their glowing colours,
He made their tiny wings.

All things bright and beautiful,
All creatures great and small,

All things wise and wonderful,
The Lord God made them all.

The rich man in his castle,
The poor man at his gate,

God made them, high or lowly,
And ordered their estate.

All things bright and beautiful,
All creatures great and small,

All things wise and wonderful,
The Lord God made them all.

The purple-headed mountain,
The river running by,

The sunset and the morning,
That brightens up the sky.

All things bright and beautiful,
All creatures great and small,

All things wise and wonderful,
The Lord God made them all.

The cold wind in the winter,
The pleasant summer sun,

The ripe fruits in the garden,
He made them every one.

All things bright and beautiful,
All creatures great and small,

All things wise and wonderful,
The Lord God made them all.

The tall trees in the greenwood,
The meadows where we play,

The rushes by the water,
We gather every day.

All things bright and beautiful,
All creatures great and small,

All things wise and wonderful,
The Lord God made them all.

He gave us eyes to see them,
And lips that we might tell,

How great is God Almighty,
Who has made all things well.

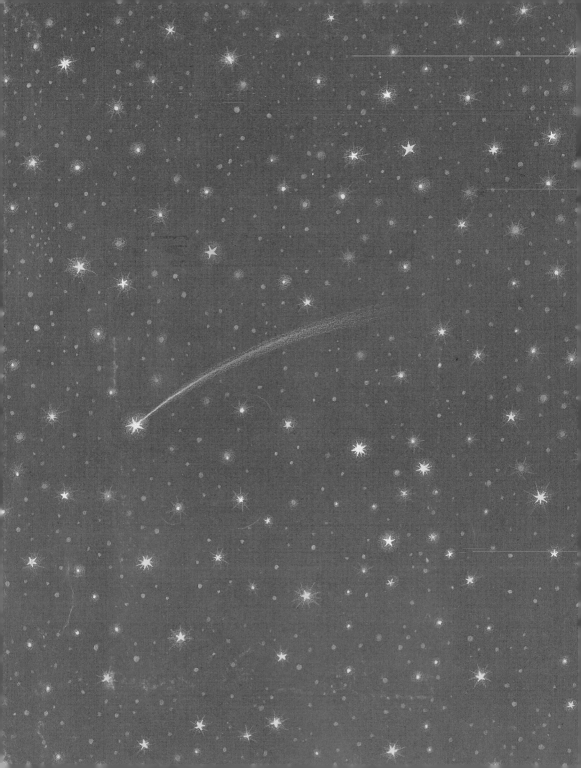